Thank you, Mr. Brown, and MERRY CHRISTMAS

Written by William A. Green • Illustrated by David R. Prehm

ISBN: 1-4392-1500-6
EAN13:9781439215005

Visit www.booksurge.com to order additional copies.

This book is dedicated to all those girls and boys, who have experienced difficulty learning, yet continue to strive to do their best.

It's also dedicated to all those teachers who dedicate their lives to teaching students with special needs.

I sat at my desk and watched out the window as the first snowflakes of winter danced to the grass-covered ground. I had countless things I needed to do. The colored Christmas lights across the street reminded me of the season. I needed to get into the holiday spirit. I needed to start a Christmas list. Of course, I needed to do lots of things.

My mind drifted back to a simpler time, when the holiday season seemed so perfect and so exciting. I thought of my wintry schooldays spent at Lamont Elementary.

M y school, nestled in the small rural town of Lamont, was a small, stately brick building built in the 1930s by men during the Great Depression. Its tall chimney reached skyward on the south side of the attached gymnasium. Two sets of large double doors welcomed us each day, and a tall flag pole with both the United States and our state flag adorned the front school yard. An iron pipe fence separated the school boundary from the street. Towering white pine trees lined the snow-covered street leading past the school and adjoining ball diamond. Each year the stately fir tree on the front lawn was decorated with Christmas lights by the 6th grade class.

N ine squatty, yellow buses, each carrying 30 to 40 students, arrived each school-day morning at nearly eight o'clock. Before the morning bell rang we all gathered on the playground. This time of year we were bundled up with heavy coats, hats, mittens, scarves, and gloves. Boots seemed to be an option for some of the older kids. We placed our books and lunch pails by the school, and scanned the playground for the largest patch of ice. Once this was found, we polished the snow from it with our mittens and gloves, and began to slide. The goal was to see who could run and slide the fastest and farthest without falling down.

Soon the bell would ring, and into the warm building we would go. Single file, of course. Stamping our boots and shaking the snow off our outer garments. Making quite a mess for Janitor George.

On this particular day, delicious smells wafted through-out the building from the Christmas dinner the cooks worked so hard to prepare. This was a time when the potatoes had to be peeled, whole turkeys had to be roasted, and the buns had to be baked from scratch. The smell of a Christmas feast was in the air.

The long hallways were all decorated with each grade's Christmas artwork. Green triangular Christmas trees cut from construction paper, red Santa faces accented with white cotton beards, and glittery angels covered the walls.

Christmas carols rang down the hall from Mr. Clark's music room in preparation for the annual Christmas program.

ach room had a real Christmas tree that smelled of the season. All were decorated with old, unwanted ornaments brought from each of our homes. There were also homemade garlands made of red and green construction paper. Some classes made the traditional popcorn garlands strung on fishing line.

Even though it was ages ago, I could still remember all those who touched my life there. Janitor George, the cooks—Mrs. Helms, Mrs. Scovel, and Nellie Richmond—Harvey my bus driver, and Mrs. Sage, my fourth grade teacher. I also thought fondly of Mr. Brown, who helped me for several years with reading and math.

Mr. Brown was my favorite teacher. He always had a smile and a friendly chuckle whenever I arrived at his door. ***"Well, look who's here. It's Miss Nancy! It's been awhile... maybe a day?"*** Then he'd smile.

Mr. Brown didn't seem that old, but his hair was kind of silver—maybe even white. He wore glasses, although I don't know why. He always looked over them when he looked you in the eye. He always wore suspenders and a white shirt and tie, and he looked rather sporty. At this time of year, he wore a Christmas tie featuring a picture of Santa, who kind of looked like Mr. Brown, only a little more portly.

Even though books were stacked to the ceiling and papers lay in large precarious piles, Mr. Brown's room was rather cozy and inviting. A large regulator clock, a calendar, an American flag, and a picture of George Washington adorned his walls. His large oak wooden desk faced the door. His old, weathered, squeaky oak chair not only swiveled, but rocked.

Mr. Brown's room was small—not much bigger than an over-sized closet. One large window faced the north, overlooking Pine Street. A small radiator hissed away beneath the window. I spent much of my time in the center of the room, seated at a small clean wooden table with four straight-backed chairs. I worked with Mr. Brown an hour each day. One half hour on reading, and one half hour on math.

It was a special class for those who had trouble with reading and math. Everyone referred to Mr. Brown's class as "Special Reading" or "Special Math." Some said it sarcastically, as though it were a place to avoid, and those who went there were dumb.

Mr. Brown, however, described his class differently. He said it was a class for "special" people—special people whose lessons had to be taught in a different way because they thought differently than others. For them, learning was a bit harder, but they certainly were not dumb. Their difficulties were just hurdles to overcome.

When I started, I had my doubts about what Mr. Brown thought. As each day passed, working on phonics and math, I began to realize that Mr. Brown was different. He tried to make learning fun. He'd reward me with praise, compliments, and an occasional piece of candy whenever I reached a goal. He'd even play Christmas music quietly on his old radio when the holidays drew near.

Mr. Brown would often ask about my family, if time allowed. He took an interest in what I had to say. He liked to hear about our plans for Christmas, who we'd have over for dinner, and how much we'd have to eat. He'd ask about my older brother Johnny's basketball team—how many points they scored and how many teams they'd beat.

Sometimes Mr. Brown would talk briefly about fishing or hunting, which were his favorite hobbies. He'd tell me about the fish he'd caught, how big they were, and what bait or lure he'd used to catch them. I learned he had a hunting dog named Dodger that could smell pheasants from the car window. I learned a *little* about Mr. Brown, and by the end of my days in his class, he knew a *lot* about me.

The day before Christmas vacation, in my fourth grade year, I didn't go to see Mr. Brown at my usual time. I had graduated, Mrs. Sage announced. Graduated?! Many other kids might have jumped for joy, knowing that they no longer had to go to "Special Reading" or "Special Math." I felt no joy, however. Instead, I tried to swallow the lump in my throat, and sat at my desk stunned. My two o'clock time with Mr. Brown would now be filled by another "special" someone.

I stopped by Mr. Brown's room at the end of that day. As I entered his doorway, tears rolled down my face. Of course, Mr. Brown greeted me in his usual way. *"Well, look who's here. It's Miss Nancy! It's been awhile… maybe a day?!"* Then he smiled. *"From the look on your face, I'm guessing you're feeling a little glum. You're probably going to miss our time together. It's been a lot of work, but we did share some fun."* Then he smiled.

All I could do was nod.

M r. Brown continued. *"Remember when I told you that you were "special"? With your effort and desire to do your best, I knew that this day would surely come. Your grades in math and reading aren't perfect, but B's are better than C's, and C's are better than D's. You are now doing far above average. But even more important than grades is your desire to achieve."* He paused briefly. *"It's really what's in your heart. If it's in your heart to be a scientist, be a scientist. If it's in your heart to be a doctor, be a doctor. If it's in your heart to be a "stay at home" Mom who raises a wonderful family, you can do that, too. My job is done. Your lessons are complete. You have now gained confidence, and have the tools to succeed."*

Mr. Brown then turned to his desk, pulled open his right bottom drawer, and retrieved a small box carefully wrapped in Christmas paper. The package was tied with a plaid ribbon, and there was a green homemade bow on top. He slid the box across the top of his cluttered desk.

"Go ahead and open it," he said.

I nside was a candy cane, a new Number 2 pencil, and a Washington Delicious apple. These were typical teacher gifts any student might expect. Beneath them was a piece of paper laying face down. I took it out and turned it over. It was a diploma. It looked pretty important, and I don't even remember what the official words read.

Ｂut I do remember this: a small tear on Mr. Brown's cheek before he said, *"Congratulations, Miss Nancy! You've graduated! You're at the top of my list. I am as proud of you as any teacher can get. You've become someone "very special"—"very special" indeed. Merry Christmas to you, and say hi to your family."*

T he bell rang. It was time to go. I jumped up and gave Mr. Brown a quick, teary hug. ***"Thank you, Mr. Brown, and Merry Christmas,"*** I said.

I placed the gifts in my lunch pail, and tucked the diploma in my pocket. Down the hall I ran, down the sidewalk, and onto my squatty yellow bus. There was no more time for tears and making a fuss. After all, it was the start of a long-awaited Christmas vacation. There were cookies to bake, ice cream to freeze, presents to wrap, and soon there would be lots of friends and family to greet.

I never saw Mr. Brown much the rest of that year. But I did see students filing through his door. I heard him chuckle and greet them one by one. I'm sure they were each special in their own way, and Mr. Brown made sure they knew it. After all, making them feel special was no doubt why he chose to become a teacher.

We moved to a neighboring town at the end of that year. I never saw Mr. Brown again. I often think of him, though, and that small tear on his cheek. To this day I wonder if he knows how he touched my life, how special he made me feel. I truly learned my reading and math lessons from Mr. Brown; but the greatest lesson I learned came from the heart... from Mr. Brown's heart to mine.

I didn't choose to become a scientist, or a doctor. I chose to become a teacher—a "special" teacher. A teacher who hopefully makes students feel special, as special as Mr. Brown did me.

W ell, so much for the wonderful memory. Snow has now covered the ground. I've got to get back to work. I have a lot of papers to check for a lot of special kids. I'll get to that Christmas list later. Besides, it's not what's on the list that makes Christmas special. It's what's in your heart that makes Christmas special. It's what's in your heart that can make anything or anyone special. I learned that from someone "very special"—"very special" indeed!

"Thank you, Mr. Brown, and **MERRY CHRISTMAS.**"

The End

For more information about the author and illustrator go to

www.greenstreetgifts.com.